Pondering
the Proverbs

What in the World Was King Solomon Thinking?

RAY SANDERS

LUCIDBOOKS

To my love and my children:

There is no missing the love that King David had for his son, King Solomon. He poured his life into his heir apparent. As a result, the boy became a man, and the man became one of the wisest kings to ever live. Neither king was perfect. Each had their flaws. Their lives were full of triumph and tragedy. It is my hope that this little book of ponderings will serve as a reminder of the love I have for each of you. I pray that it will serve as a reminder that though men may fail you, the wisdom of the Lord can be trusted as a guide for living life to the fullest. A heritage is what we are given. A legacy is what we leave. May the insights on the pages that follow serve as a gift that illuminates our family's path for generations to come.

"Let those with understanding receive guidance by exploring the meaning in these proverbs."
—Proverbs 1:5–6

These are the proverbs of Solomon, David's son, king of Israel. Their purpose is to teach people wisdom and discipline, to help them understand the insights of the wise. Their purpose is to teach people to live disciplined and successful lives, to help them do what is right, just, and fair. These proverbs will give insight to the simple, knowledge and discernment to the young. Let the wise listen to these proverbs and become even wiser. Let those with understanding receive guidance by exploring the meaning in these proverbs and parables, the words of the wise and their riddles.
—Proverbs 1:2–6

Table of Contents

Preface

The book of Proverbs has changed my life; I am who I am in big part due to the insights I have gained from King Solomon and his friends.

Pondering the Proverbs is the second in a series of books that encourage readers to slow down and consider teachings from leaders of the past. It all started with Pondering the Parables in which readers were encouraged to sit at the feet of Jesus and consider his principles and teachings. Pondering the Proverbs is available for readers like you to explore as we consider together what in the world King Solomon was thinking when he assembled his little book on wisdom.

I am amazed that the God of the universe has taken interest in us and provided us with many insights about how He thinks and operates. He is knowable and desires to be known. I believe it is in our pondering on His Word that He meets with us and shares great insights on living life to the fullest.

Solomon had many friends and family members that he no doubt loved and cared for and hoped to influence with all that he had learned in life. That too is my desire with this book. I am no Solomon, but I am happy to share what I have learned with all who care to listen.

INTRODUCTION:

What in the World Was King Solomon Thinking?

Proverbs is a book of wisdom. For centuries it has stood the test of time. Although the book is thousands of years old, the wisdom of Proverbs remains relevant now more than ever.

King David was the courageous and most beloved king of Israel; yet his son Solomon is considered the wisest king of all. Although Solomon is not the sole author of the book of Proverbs, he is believed to be the curator of the body of work. The opening chapter clearly credits Solomon as the primary author and collector of the proverbs when it says, *"These are the proverbs of Solomon son of David, king of Israel"* (Proverbs 1:1).

The book of Proverbs serves as a deep well of wisdom from which to draw guidance for life and work. There is hardly a topic that it does not touch on or relate to. Perhaps one of the best-known passages is found in Proverbs 3:5–6: *"Trust in the LORD with all your heart do not depend on your own understanding. Seek*

1

his will in all you do, and he will show you which path to take."
Where does such wisdom come from? Kings and queens would
travel from near and far to sit in Solomon's presence and marvel
at his vast knowledge, experience, and wisdom.

We know for certain that King David invested in his heir
apparent. David had asked God's permission to build the Lord's
temple. Although building the temple would have been an
honorable task, God had destined that privilege for another,
David's son, King Solomon. the Lord desired that David spend
more time building into the life of the boy than being distracted
with the task of temple-building. Clearly, the time he spent with
Solomon was time well-spent.

Proverbs 3:5–6 has been my life verse for as long as I can
remember. In good times and bad, that passage has served as a
reminder of where my strength comes from. It is a reminder that
no matter what comes my way, the Lord of the book of Proverbs
can be trusted to see me through.

I believe so much in the relevance and power of the book of
Proverbs that I have every new client read at least one chapter a
day for thirty-one days. Many of my clients read and refer to the
book of Proverbs as their guiding principles for life. *Pondering
the Proverbs* contains but a small fraction of the lessons and
insights I have gleaned from the book of Proverbs. I have read it
many times over the years, and the lessons I have learned never
cease to inspire me.

What in the world was Solomon thinking when he compiled
such a beautiful body of literature? Somehow, I believe that
Solomon knew this would be his greatest gift to humanity. He
was not a perfect man, and he failed to practice some of the

wisdom he compiled. But that does not make the wisdom any less true. It only reminds us how much we benefit when we take the time to ponder the pages in this ancient book of wisdom, the book of Proverbs.

My hope is that, in some small way, *Pondering the Proverbs* will serve as a catalyst to raise up Proverbs enthusiasts for years to come. Come now and join me as we ponder the proverbs together.

CHAPTER 1:

The Fool's Failing Formulas

I sat in my algebra class with a glazed look on my face. The teacher stood at the front of the classroom with his back to the students scratching formulas on a blackboard with chalk remnants pressed between his fingers. He was teaching, but hardly anyone was learning; his formulas were failing.

Information spewed from his mouth like water from a fire hydrant. Students gathered around him attempting to catch any insight they could regarding the numbers, letters, dashes, and slashes that appeared at lightning speed before their eyes. The instructor appeared to be proud of his ability to espouse knowledge. He continued to wave his arms, dot his i's and cross his t's, but the wisdom of his words was lost on his audience.

It is one thing to gain knowledge and experience; it is another to apply it properly to life. Wisdom is the ability to apply what we have learned as we navigate the challenges and opportunities of life. It is not enough to know. We must learn to apply what we know to life; doing so makes us wise.

Information has never been more available or accessible than it is today. The internet can make us subject matter experts overnight. For example, one of my sons recently shared that he could learn what I knew about a certain topic in a matter of minutes by doing a simple online search. To some extent, he was right. However, acquiring knowledge does not guarantee that he would know how to use or apply what he had learned. That ability comes through experience and wisdom.

Solomon's goal was to provide insight into the benefits of gaining wisdom, instruction, and understanding. By doing so, his readers would gain prudence, discretion, and guidance for life. In essence, they would gain the ability to apply what they had learned to life. Oh, I wish that my algebra teacher had read Proverbs; perhaps he would have learned that knowledge is not enough. We must learn to apply what we have learned to life. When we do, we become wise.

Solomon strongly believed that fools despise instruction and wisdom. He believed that the way of the fool leads to failing formulas, whereas the way of the wise leads to life at its fullest. The wisdom of Solomon was no doubt rooted in his commitment to being a lifelong learner.

> *They rejected my advice and paid no attention when I corrected them. Therefore, they must eat the bitter fruit of living their own way, choking on their own schemes. For simpletons turn away from me—to death. Fools are destroyed by their own complacency. But all who listen to me will live in peace, untroubled by fear of harm.*
> —Proverbs 1:30–33

PAUSE AND PONDER:
RECORD YOUR REFLECTIONS AND PERSONAL INSIGHTS.

How about you? What is your attitude toward learning? Do you remain open to learning new things? How are you gaining knowledge and insight that enriches your perspectives? How have you learned to apply those insights to life? Doing so will not only make you smart; it will also make you wise.

CHAPTER 2:

Knuckle Busting

There is a rite of passage that happens between a father and his son. For years a man is accompanied by his boy in all kinds of scenarios. The lad watches in wonder as his daddy performs seemingly amazing acts of strength, fixes anything that is broken, and protects when things become less than safe.

The relationship between father and son is the perfect picture of an apprenticeship. The dad works, and the boy watches. The dad works, and the boy helps. The boy works, and the dad helps. The boy masters, and the dad celebrates. Thus, the apprentice completes his rite of passage.

Not so long ago one of my boys was determined to make a repair on his vehicle. He asked to borrow my tools. I obliged, and he went about knuckle busting and making the repair. After considerable time, I decided to check on his progress knowing that normally the fix would not have taken so long.

As I approached the apprentice at work, it was clear to me what needed to be done. I asked if I could help. My helpfulness was met with a determined face. My advice was not welcomed. An independent spirit was set on self-sufficiency.

Out of respect for his desire to prevail, I smiled and walked away. I watched from a window as my son buried his head under the hood, failing time and again to make the fix.

The writer of Proverbs shares great advice for moments like these. He encourages us to receive and treasure words of wisdom as we incline our hearts to understanding. That is, when the student is ready, the teacher will appear. The key to obtaining timely success often depends on how quickly we are willing to accept input and advice.

It was painful to watch the prolonged struggle as my son all but crawled on top of his engine as he attempted to prove his abilities and master the challenge. As darkness fell on the shade-tree mechanic, I approached the vehicle a second time. I noticed a new expression on my son's face. He was tired, worn-out, and exasperated. He was so close, yet so far. Finally, he had a willingness and openness for input and advice.

I shared a few thoughts, encouraged him to carry on, and soon after I made it back inside the house, the sound of the engine firing up made me smile. He had done it and on his terms. I admired his drive and determination and was proud he made the fix. This also reminded me of my own apprenticeship. I recalled that at times, I had experienced unnecessary and prolonged struggle because I failed to reach out sooner rather than later. Sometimes, asking and receiving advice from others and the Lord could have saved me a lot of time, energy, and frustration.

There is true wisdom in a willingness to remain teachable with a heart inclined to learning. The Lord is willing, but He will not force His way upon us. Like a dad desiring to help his strong-willed son, He is willing to wait and let us help ourselves until we are willing to humble ourselves and accept His wisdom.

The next time you find yourself in a bit of a pickle, consider the proverbs as they encourage us to value and seek wisdom as we remain open to advice with a heart inclined to learning.

> *My child, listen to what I say and treasure my commands. Tune your ears to wisdom and concentrate on understanding. Cry out for insight and ask for understanding. Search for them as you would for silver; seek them like hidden treasures. Then you will understand what it means to fear the LORD, and you will gain knowledge of God. For the LORD grants wisdom! From his mouth come knowledge and understanding. He grants a treasure of common sense to the honest. He is a shield to those who walk with integrity. He guards the paths of the just and protects those who are faithful to him. Then you will understand what is right, just, and fair and you will find the right way to go.*
>
> —Proverbs 2:1–9

PAUSE AND PONDER:
RECORD YOUR REFLECTIONS AND PERSONAL INSIGHTS.

How about you? Are you open to advice, input, and correction? What if the insight comes from someone with less experience? Are you willing to humble yourself and receive the words that could serve as a game changer?

CHAPTER 3:

Trust or Thrust?

As a young couple, my wife and I started our lives together living in Washington, DC. We were wide-eyed kids from Oklahoma adjusting to life in a large metropolitan city. My days working at the United States Senate shaped me for years to come.

During the holidays, we would often make the drive back to our roots as we navigated the highways and byways that led us home. We relied on foldable paper maps and road signs to get us there. It was especially challenging when traveling at night. One misstep and you could soon find yourself miles away from your desired destination. This was long before cell phones and GPS navigation systems were available.

More than once, we found ourselves pulled over on the side of the road scratching our heads trying to decide whether we were on the right path. Do we trust the map, or do we trust our instincts? Let's just say that the maps were always right!

Proverbs gives us insight on how to handle such predicaments; the writer encourages us to trust in the Lord and not to lean too much on our own understanding (Proverbs 3:5–6). When we trust Him, we will remain on the right path and find ourselves at the right location.

In a world where information is king, relying on logic, facts, and experience can become the norm. It is not that we should ignore the obvious, but a little further reading in Proverbs 3 reveals the key to success: Acknowledge the Lord in all your ways, and He will direct your path. What was the king getting at?

Proverbs 3:5–6 reminds us that not only do we have the Word of God as our road map for navigating life, but we also have the Holy Spirit as our tour guide. Acknowledge Him, and He will help us interpret the map, navigate the changing landscape of life, and direct our steps along the way. The catch? We must be willing to read the map and listen for the still, small whisper of our guide.

> *Trust in the LORD with all your heart do not depend on your own understanding. Seek his will in all you do, and he will show you which path to take.*
> —Proverbs 3:5–6

PAUSE AND PONDER:
RECORD YOUR REFLECTIONS AND PERSONAL INSIGHTS.

How about you? What is guiding your life? Are you like a Wild West pioneer wandering across the countryside in search for a pot of gold? Or are you willing to trust an experienced guide who can keep you on track and heading in the right direction? The choice is yours. You can trust the Lord, or you can thrust yourself into the great unknown, alone.

CHAPTER 4:

Boys to Men

Fathers tend to have their own way of communicating with their sons. Their style tends to be direct and to the point. King Solomon referred to this approach as instruction as contrasted with a mother's method of teaching.

The father's instruction was short on narrative and nurture. It focused more on see as I do, and do as I do. The father's ways were more caught than taught. Whereas a mother's approach to teaching might be more deliberate, involved, and coddling, the father's way of instructing was rooted in the art of apprenticeship.

Growing up in a farming community, I saw a father's leadership style played out in living color. As a dad walked and worked the fields, his boys were ever at his side observing, watching, and doing. Few words passed between them, but plenty of learning took place. This was the epitome of on-the-job-training. Sink or swim. You were handed a hoe and told to start chopping. Other than an occasional rebuke, you were hired, and the pay was nothing more than room and board.

There is a softer side in King Solomon's writings. He references the tenderness of the boy. He acknowledges that his son is young, vulnerable, and underdeveloped. It would be easy to expect too much too soon. He understands the importance of fathers remembering their sons are boys, not the men they will become.

The father's instruction, training, and mentorship must be palatable, relatable, and on the level of the learner. The instruction should be challenging but not condescending, pushing the limits but not breaking the spirt—all while developing and transferring skill sets, experience, and expertise with timely finesse. There is method to the so-called madness of raising boys to be men. The outcomes speak for themselves. A boy is transformed as the age-appropriate instruction has its effect.

To be taught is to be led. To teach is to lead. Through the father's instruction, the son observes and is shown the way. As the father shows the way, the boy grows and matures. The lessons are taught and caught as the boy becomes a man.

The proverbs value the importance of instruction and teaching. Both have their place. It is left up to us to determine the timing and method to be used as we encourage growth and development of those we love and lead.

My children listen when your father corrects you. Pay attention and learn good judgment, for I am giving you good guidance. Don't turn away from my instructions. For I too was once my father's son, tenderly loved as my mother's only child. My father taught me, "Take my words to heart. Follow my commands, and you will live. Get wisdom; develop good judgment. Don't forget my words or turn away from them. Don't turn your back on wisdom, for she will protect you. Love her, and she will guard you. Getting wisdom is the wisest thing you can do! And whatever else you do develop good judgment. If you prize wisdom, she will make you great. Embrace her, and she will honor you. She will place a lovely wreath on your head; she will present you with a beautiful crown." My child, listen to me and do as I say, and you will have a long, good life. I will teach you wisdom's ways and lead you in straight paths. When you walk, you won't be held back, when you run, you won't stumble. Take hold of my instructions; don't let them go. Guard them, for they are the key to life.

—Proverbs 4:1–13

PAUSE AND PONDER:
RECORD YOUR REFLECTIONS AND PERSONAL INSIGHTS.

How about you? How are you leading others in your life? Are you considering the appropriate method for dealing with the learner? Are you a leader that others desire to follow as your ways are caught and put into practice?

CHAPTER 5:

The Attraction of Distraction

There is hardly a man who hasn't, in some way, been attracted and distracted by the physical appearance of a beautiful woman. In her presence, he turns to mush. He loses his better judgment. She has an influence on him that is hard to overcome. When the attraction is motivated by love, it becomes a powerful bond. When the attraction is driven by lust, it becomes a bind.

King Solomon understood the lure of attraction to be a distraction. He used the draw between a man and a woman to illustrate the power of temptation to derail our journey. Temptation comes in many forms. Certainly, the sultry eyes of a mysterious woman have led many a man down a regrettable path. The love of money has ruined countless marriages, friendships, and relationships. The desire for power has crushed intimacy, growth, and purpose for many leaders. The perceived advantage of taking a shortcut sometimes leads to an even longer wait. The list of distractions is lengthy.

All of us can recall someone who started out strong with unprecedented potential. Everything they did seemed to turn out right. For them, success became the norm. But suddenly, with one simple decision or one misstep, the lure of temptation put them in a bind that forever altered their course in life.

What might have been never comes to fruition because the attraction and distraction left them in traction. Their story had a different ending than anyone would have imagined. In an instant, they succumbed to temptation, and the lasting effects must be endured for a lifetime. Regret sets in as they consider what could have been. The person they had hoped to be is now a part of their past.

How did it happen? How did someone, seemingly so strong, end up being so weak? Proverbs tells us such compromise happened subtly. Compromise creeped in. They started removing disciplines and safeguard as they became numb to warning signs and reproof. They slowly lowered their guard, and their standards faded like the mist of the morning dew.

How can you resist and overcome the attraction of distraction? There is a powerful and persuasive temptation that wrestles inside the heart and mind of every man. It is ever-present patiently waiting for the slip, the compromise, and the faulty decision that violates his better judgment and leads to ruin.

The words of the ancient king ring true: *"Mockers hate to be corrected, so they stay away from the wise. A glad heart makes a happy face; a broken heart crushes the spirit. A wise person is hungry for knowledge, while the fool feeds on trash"* (Proverbs 15:12–14).

There is still time. Hear his warning. Take control. Get back on track before you take the turn down a dead-end road with no option of turning back.

> *For the lips of an immoral woman are sweet as honey, and her mouth is smoother than oil. But in the end she is bitter as poison, as dangerous as a double-edged sword. Her feet go down to death; her steps lead straight to the grave.*
>
> —Proverbs 5:3–5

PAUSE AND PONDER:
RECORD YOUR REFLECTIONS AND PERSONAL INSIGHTS.

How about you? What stronghold lingers in the shadows waiting to take advantage when your guard is lowered? As the temptation simmers beneath the surface, out of sight but not out of mind, will it swallow you and pull you down and away from all you have become and are meant to be?

CHAPTER 6:

The Ensuring and Enduring Ant

More than once in my life I have been caught off guard by a seemingly innocent den of red fire ants. Those little mounds of red dirt appear at various locations throughout the prairie with no rhyme or reason. For the most part, red ants, which are capable of carrying multiple times their body weight, go about their day minding their own business. But beware of making the mistake of standing too close to a fire ant mound.

Let's just say there is a reason for describing someone who is impatient as having ants in their pants. An unfortunate encounter with fire ants literally gives one a reason for dancing as the unwilling host will do everything possible to shake themselves free of the venomous ant stings that dance across the skin. Once the biting begins, clothes start flying. The pain is excruciating and relentless. The cute little creatures that have a heart for work, possess a fighting nature that weakens foes hundreds of times their size.

Despite their reputation as creatures to be avoided, among themselves, fire ants are very social beings that cooperate with each other and work hard to build nests by pushing up soil as they shape underground tunnels. They are drawn to open, sunny areas, such as meadows, pastures, parks, playgrounds, lawns, and golf courses.

Like workers at a factory, fire ants work in shifts. In the morning and evening, they scavenge for food. The hunters bring back morsels for the queen, larvae, and other workers. Living in an ant den requires a lot of work as a fire ant colony can grow up to 150 mounds, housing more than seven million ants per acre.

No doubt the writer of Proverbs had a fond appreciation for the ant. He surely had a healthy respect for their militant capabilities, but it was their work ethic that caught his attention. He encourages us to consider the way of the ant and, in so doing, grow wise.

Without a leader or ruler, the ant prepares in season, gathering what is needed for harder times ahead. The ant is prudent and considers challenges, threats, and risks that are certain to come. The ant doesn't live in fear but minds its own business, takes responsibility for its actions, pulls far more than its own weight, and delivers like clockwork. If threatened, it will do whatever is necessary to protect and serve the purpose of the colony. The ant is self-motivated and built to survive.

How about you? Are you prepared? No, you are not to live in worry. But are you doing what you can today to prepare for tomorrow? It has been said that you can "pay me now or pay me later." Staying diligent about our work, saving what we can, and protecting our efforts ensures that when the harder times come, we are certain to endure. Such is the way of the ant.

Yes, we do well to keep our distance from fire ants, but if we are careful, we can glean wisdom from their ways.

> *Take a lesson from the ants, you lazybones. Learn from their ways and become wise! Though they have no prince or governor or ruler to make them work, they labor hard all summer, gathering food for the winter. But you, lazybones, how long will you sleep? When will you wake up? A little extra sleep, a little more slumber, a little folding of the hands to rest- then poverty will pounce on you like a bandit; scarcity will attack you like an armed robber.*
>
> —Proverbs 6:6–11

PAUSE AND PONDER:
RECORD YOUR REFLECTIONS AND PERSONAL INSIGHTS.

How about you? What can you observe and learn from the world around you? How is the creator of the universe speaking to you through His creation, large and small?

CHAPTER 7:

The Haunting Reminder

There is a drive within a man that is intended for love and procreation. When left undisciplined or unsatisfied, this drive often leads him to seek a substitution for what is best.

Sometimes, through naivety and at other times, with full intent, he finds himself in the presence of a neglected woman, aching from a lack of love and seeking to ease her pain in the arms of a man who will hold her close for a short time.

Like two strangers looking for love in all the wrong places, her seductive speech persuades him and lures him into a fantasy he has played out time and again in his mind. Her smooth talk acts as a salve to his lonely heart. She compels him and, like an ox led to slaughter, he gives way, giving no account to the price he will pay for his temporary act of passion, which will cost him more than the time he commits to relieve his pain.

This story has played out in many ways throughout history. An untamed sexual drive overwhelms one's better judgment and in short order, the innocence of a pure life is consumed and tainted for a lifetime. Years ago, such acts of self-medication were only fulfilled in person or in the mind of the one succumbed to the temptation.

Today, isolation and the digital age grant access to countless opportunities to visualize whatever fantasy comes to mind. Although not done in person, these acts are as real to the mind as they are to the fiber of the soul. Images forever captured and burned into the memory are unrelenting and unwilling to let go. They remain a haunting reminder of a moment of weakness in pursuit of passing pleasure.

Unfortunately, for many, this pattern becomes an addiction, a constant distraction to everyday life. It ruins relationships and the hope of overcoming the stronghold of pornography, sexual promiscuity, and perversion. The trap is set, and the victim is held captive in a self-inflicted prison of deception.

Proverbs speaks of man's tendency to give way to sexual urges, a temptation that is not easily overcome. The writer warns of the trouble and pain that will result when compromise is accepted. He urges his readers not to allow their hearts to turn aside or to be led down the road of seduction.

His advice is not easy to take, especially when heartache and passion are the motivators. Yet, not allowing ourselves to go near the road of destruction is the key. Don't go there. Avoid the turn in the road. Silence the temptation that competes for your attention and replace it with words of wisdom that have often guided your life. Remember, many victims have wandered down this path. Forbid yourself from being found among their ranks.

God never said the narrow way would be easy. The idea that it should be easy to avoid compromise is a modern man-made mindset. Remember that there is no guarantee of comfort in our calling. God calls us to do hard things. Why? Because He strengthens our backs; He doesn't lighten our load. In the end, we come out stronger.

> *I saw some naive young men, and one in particular who lacked common sense. He was crossing the street near the house of an immoral woman, strolling down the path by her house. It was at twilight, in the evening, as deep darkness fell. The woman approached him, seductively dressed and sly of heart. She was the brash, rebellious type, never content to stay at home. She is often in the streets and markets, soliciting at every corner. She threw her arms around him and kissed him, and with a brazen look she said, "I've just made my peace offerings and fulfilled my vows. You're the one I was looking for! I came out to find you, and here you are! My bed is spread with beautiful blankets, with colored sheets of Egyptian linen. I've perfumed my bed with myrrh, aloes, and cinnamon. Come, let's drink our fill of love until morning. Let's enjoy each other's caresses, for my husband is not home. He's away on a long trip. He has taken a wallet full of money with him and won't return until later this month." So, she seduced him with her pretty speech and enticed him with her flattery. He followed her at once, like an ox going to the slaughter. He was like a stag caught in a trap, awaiting the arrow that would pierce its heart. He was like a bird flying into a snare, little knowing it would cost him his life.*
>
> —Proverbs 7:7–23

PAUSE AND PONDER:
RECORD YOUR REFLECTIONS AND PERSONAL INSIGHTS.

How about you? What temptations are you often presented with? How do you seek to overcome these strongholds? Who do you trust and share your challenges with? Seek out someone who can help hold you accountable and encourage you to do what is best.

CHAPTER 8:

Mustard Syndrome

L ooking in all the wrong places. It never fails. I stand in front of the refrigerator with the door wide open. I look. I shuffle and rearrange. Try as I might, the mustard eludes me.

Giving up, I look to my wife for assistance. Without fail, she approaches the array of refrigerated goods and upon her arrival, the mustard leaps off the shelf and into her hand! She claims I suffer from mustard syndrome. I think she might be right.

That's not exactly how it goes, but it sure feels like she has some sort of homing device that takes her right to where the mustard is hiding out in the open! I still contend it has to do with a heights advantage. It just seems everything is eye level for her, whereas, for me, it is always like looking for a needle in a haystack.

Sometimes, my search for the Lord and the mustard have had the same result. Try as I might He remains elusive, hidden, and nowhere to be found even though He is available in plain sight. Why is it that some people can find God whenever they need him, and I often feel lost and alone?

We get a clue about my dilemma from Proverbs. The issue isn't that the Lord won't be found; the issue is that I am looking in all the wrong places. All too often, we look for the Lord on our terms and according to our ways. We look for wisdom by other means and other ways when the answer waits before us in plain sight. The point is clear: Those who seek Him will find Him. It may take effort, and it might require bending our knees to get on the right level, but He will be found.

There is a blessing for those who find Him and listen to Him as they begin life with each new day. Whoever finds Him finds life, but to find Him, we must look in the right place. When we do, He will be found. In fact, He wants to be found. He does not hide His face. He makes every effort to be found be us. The issue is not with who is hiding but rather who is looking.

My wife has a knack for looking in the right place. She never fails to find the mustard. I'm starting to rely on her less as I bend my knees and reach for the very thing I've been looking for. It was there all along waiting to be found.

Wisdom isn't hiding. Those who search for wisdom will find it. Wisdom is crying out. Watch for it. Wisdom shows up with insight, knowledge, understanding, and discernment in all kinds of ways. There's no limit to the ways in which wisdom is revealed. Certainly, wisdom is found in the Word and during times of worship, prayer, and meditation, but wisdom is also found in the street. Wisdom cries out in the world around us. Circumstances, happenings, divine appointments, revelations, and relationships are but a few of the ways that wisdom tries to gain our attention.

Be alert. Be attentive. Expect wisdom to speak. The key is to be listening for that still, small voice and staying so close in our walk with God that even His whisper gains our attention. He is waiting to greet you. You will discover that He hasn't been hiding at all. In fact, He is doing all that he can to gain your attention and be found by you. He loves being found, especially by people like you—people who are searching for Him with all their hearts.

> *And so, my children, listen to me, for all who follow my ways are joyful. Listen to my instruction and be wise. Don't ignore it. Joyful are those who listen to me, watching for me daily at my gates, waiting for me outside my home! For whoever finds me finds life and receives favor from the LORD. But those who miss me injure themselves. All who hate me love death.*
> —Proverbs 8:32–36

PAUSE AND PONDER:
RECORD YOUR REFLECTIONS AND PERSONAL INSIGHTS.

How about you? Are you looking for what you want and desire in all the wrong places? Has your frustration grown as you continue to come up empty-handed? Maybe it's time to bend your knees, say a prayer, and ask the Lord to lead you where He can be found.

CHAPTER 9:

The Fool's Persona

If we are not careful, we can waste a lot of time debating and engaging with a fool. We have better things to do than to waste effort and energy on someone who mocks our beliefs or violates our values.

I recently attended a large college sporting event with more than 85,000 people in attendance. The crowd was loud and energetic. Three rows behind me, no less than 100 feet from the playing field, a man, lacking self-awareness, screamed profanities at the players and gave unrelenting advice and senseless critiques to the coaches.

His voice was drowned out by the cheers and applause of those who surrounded him. With no regard for the countless looks of displeasure that he received from other fans, he continued to play the fool as a proverbial armchair quarterback. Despite many requests for him to hang up his antics, he didn't budge as he did his best to make everyone around him regret his presence as they considered the possibility of not renewing their season tickets.

The proverb is right: "*Whoever corrects a scoffer gets himself abuse*" (Proverbs 9:7). Having to endure the jeers of a fanatical sports fan can turn even the most exciting event into a bowl of misery. Hardly anything is more annoying than a loud-mouthed obnoxious fool. What they lack in knowledge, they try to make up for with noise. Certainly, a raised voice is a sign of a low emotional intelligence.

Contrast the fool's persona with that of a wise man who quietly goes about his business listening and taking instruction as needed. He is admired and considered to be a good man who increases in learning.

Proverbs consistently points out the benefits of listening and learning. One benefit of gaining wisdom, knowledge, and understanding is a longer and more enjoyable life. Conversely, a babbling fool's influence is cut short because he talks when he should be listening; he gains nothing to improve his plight and simply continues to expound the same recycled words and ideas. Where do you sit in the stadium of life? Are you a student of life and learning, or are you a know-it-all with much to say and little to gain?

Proverbs lays out a path worth following; the writer says, "*Give instruction to a wise man, and he will be still wiser; teach a righteous man, and he will increase in learning*" (Proverbs 9:9). Will you play the fool or embrace the winning ways of the wise? The choice is yours to make.

> *Anyone who rebukes a mocker will get an insult in return. Anyone who corrects the wicked will get hurt. So don't bother correcting mockers; they will only hate you. But correct the wise, and they will love you.*
> —Proverbs 9:7–8

**PAUSE AND PONDER:
RECORD YOUR REFLECTIONS AND PERSONAL INSIGHTS.**

How about you? Are you wasting your time arguing and debating with a fool? Are you making the most of your time and opportunities? Have you repeatedly tried to provide insight and perspective only to find it falling on deaf ears? If you continue to take the same approach, what result are you likely to obtain?

CHAPTER 10:

Looking Back

Growing up, I learned that my father had great intentions. He often made promises, but for whatever reason, something always seemed to come up that altered the plan. He talked about taking us to Disney World, but we ended up with a day trip to Six Flags. Fun? Sure. But let's be honest, Six Flags is not Disney World.

I am pretty sure this wasn't the way my father wanted to be remembered. But the truth is, it was the way he lived his life. He had good intentions, but as hard as it is for me to admit, my father lacked integrity. He said one thing and did another. He couldn't be counted on—to the point that his bad choices earned him the distinction of being a convicted felon.

How do you want to be remembered? Proverbs 10:7 says, *"We have happy memories of the godly."* I hope that the memories others have of me are happy ones. Although I can't make anyone happy, I can influence the memories they have of me. It pains me when I consider that I have been less than my best at times and that I have contributed to others having some less than wonderful memories of me.

Sometimes, a heartfelt apology can bridge the gap between what was and what should have been. I can live with regret, or I can determine to make up for lost time with the new opportunities I have. Certainly, some memories are influenced by false narratives, but others are brutally accurate. We can't change the past, but we can take a hard run at the future.

While we can never know exactly how we will be remembered, the best way to understand our legacy is to reflect on how we currently interact with others, the values we live by, and the positive impact we strive to make on the lives around us. Essentially, we have to consciously live by the principles that reflect the qualities and actions for which we want to be remembered when we are gone.

Here are some applicable insights:

- How you treat others: Do you show kindness, compassion, and respect in your daily interactions?
- Your values and beliefs: What are the core principles that guide your decisions and actions?
- Positive contributions: Are you actively contributing to your community, family, or field in a meaningful way?
- Relationships you build: Do you nurture meaningful connections with people and leave a positive impression on them?
- Your legacy: Are you involved in activities or causes that will continue to have an impact after you're gone?

Self-awareness is essential. Living intentionally and with an emphasis on being a positive influence in other people's lives is the key.

- **Seek feedback from others:** Ask close friends and family how they perceive you and what qualities they associate with you.
- **Reflect on your past actions:** Think about moments when you made a significant positive impact on someone's life.
- **Journaling:** Regularly write down your thoughts and aspirations about how you want to be remembered.
- **Focus on the present:** While considering your legacy is important, the most impactful way to shape how you will be remembered is by living intentionally and positively in the present.

History is made every day. It's not how we start that matters but how we finish that determines how we will be remembered. Do what you can today to create happy memories. Remember that memories last a lifetime; go make some happy memories.

We have happy memories of the godly, but the name of a wicked person rots away.

—Proverbs 10:7

PAUSE AND PONDER:
RECORD YOUR REFLECTIONS AND PERSONAL INSIGHTS.

How about you? Are you making promises you can't keep? Do you find yourself living a life of good intentions? Do you overpromise and under-deliver? Take a hint from King Solomon and determine today to walk in integrity. Be a person who can be counted on to do as you say you will do.

CHAPTER 11:

God's Economy

I stood in the checkout lane with my arms full of groceries. Yes, I should have utilized a shopping cart, but I am an overconfident man who sometimes underestimates. I was struggling to keep my grab-and-go loot under control, and the line wasn't moving! I looked like a juggling act gone bad. I was about to lose it in more ways than one. The elderly lady in front of me was taking her sweet time as she shopped with what appeared to be her grandchildren. The kids were well-behaved, and the lady seemed kind, but I was aching for an exit.

Finally, the conveyor belt cleared just enough for me to lighten my load. As I observed the slow-moving grocery shoppers, I noticed that the woman was paying with the type of food vouchers available to the underprivileged. Unfortunately, I started to judge. I looked over her purchases to see if she was abusing the system. Everything looked in order. She was only buying necessities. But why would a well-dressed kind and orderly little family need subsidy?

Like a creep, I eavesdropped and discovered the lady was in fact a grandparent; her daughter had been killed, and the children's dad was in jail. She was a hero helping out, and I was a juggling jerk.

As she reached to pay for the groceries, I stepped in and paid the bill. She looked at me and instantly started to cry. She assured me I had no idea how much difference my assistance would make. I felt it was the least I could do. I admired her courage and strength. I wanted to be more of a giver. Not just with a few bucks at the checkout counter but in every aspect of life.

So often the way God works is counterintuitive to the way we operate. Many of the sayings presented in Proverbs will make you scratch your head in wonder. If nothing else, they make you think. For example, Proverbs 11:24 says, *"Give freely and become more wealthy; be stingy and lose everything."*

But you say to yourself: I worked hard for my money. I sacrificed to get to where I am today. My retirement account needs more zeros at the end. I've got bills to pay, trips to take, and pleasures to indulge in. I earned it. It's mine, and it is meant for me. I'm not going to feel one ounce of guilt for a little self-indulgence.

Good for you. Welcome to the top of the pack. You are among the most privileged and wealthy in the world. Not only do you have disposable income, but you also have a job, a roof over your head, a car to drive, food in the cupboard, cures for your pains, and comforts to enjoy. Such is not the case for so many in the world; you drew the lucky stick. The bottom line is this: You are privileged.

You can keep it all to yourself. You can hoard it under lock and key. But what if you were given much so that you could give much. What if you were chosen because you could be trusted to share the wealth, opportunity, and love?

Am I suggesting that you go broke by giving all you own away? No! But there is a principle of generosity at play though it is counterintuitive. By the way, generosity isn't just about money. The principle applies to time, talent, and treasure. There are more ways than one to join the fun and thrill of generosity.

What if you practiced generosity by carrying a twenty-dollar bill in your wallet and constantly asked yourself who the Lord was leading you to bless with a surprise that week? The recipient probably won't be a panhandler looking to self-medicate, but it might be a sweet grandmother in a grocery store checkout line, or it might mean covering the cost of a deli sandwich for a busy executive who needs to be reminded that he should consider the joys of generosity as a way of life.

Give some thought to ways you can become more generous to those around you. Don't break the bank or sell the farm, but do be ready to crack a smile when you experience the world according to God's economy.

> *Give freely and become more wealthy; be stingy and lose everything. The generous will prosper; those who refresh others will themselves be refreshed. People curse those who hoard their grain, but they bless the one who sells in time of need. If you search for good, you will find favor; but if you search for evil, it will find you! Trust in your money and down you go! But the godly flourish like leaves in spring.*
>
> —Proverbs 11:24–28

PAUSE AND PONDER:
RECORD YOUR REFLECTIONS AND PERSONAL INSIGHTS.

How about you? Do you tend to have a generous attitude? Are you more of a giver or a taker? Do you yield the front row parking spot to a stranger? Do you clean the dishes and give your spouse the night off? Do you return your neighbor's trash dumpster to its bin?

CHAPTER 12:

Crucial Conversations

I come from a long line of hotheads; I was well trained in this behavior pattern. It nearly ruined my marriage, but more than thirty years ago, my wife set me straight. She called me out and then graciously helped me reprogram my ways. I am forever grateful for our crucial conversation. I am and continue to be a work in progress; it is more like chiseling marble than molding clay.

The tongue often goes untamed. Like a dog about to get a special treat, the tongue wags and wiggles on autopilot. All too often, what comes off the tip of our tongues is related to what has rapidly boiled to the top of our mind. If we let our thoughts simmer before we spew steam like a tea kettle over a hot flame, we would save ourselves from having some scorching conversations.

In *Crucial Conversations*, the authors explain the reason for our primal response of speaking without thinking. According to the authors, a metaphysical response takes place when we sense conflict, threats, or danger. It is rooted in the flight-or-fight response. In an instant, blood that is rich with adrenaline is rushed to the large muscles in our arms and legs. Our bodies take action and are prepared for battle or boogie. Our brains, on the other hand, give way and drop into instinct mode. We are on autopilot.[1] No wonder we question our better judgment or suffer brain fog about why things happen the way they do when we engage in conflict. We literally drain our brain of oxygen.

This might explain our tendency to launch a rapid response, but it is not a license to kill. As reasoning and thinking beings, we have the capacity to overcome our nature with choices. Habits and hang ups don't have to remain strongholds that hinder our effectiveness in relationships. Replacing poor reactions with preferred responses leads us down a new road with less regret. It will take time, but we can unlearn instinctive reactions and bring them into submission using self-control.

Proverbs 12:18 state a beautiful thing when the writer addresses to the tongue's potential to do good: *"There is one whose rash words are like sword thrusts, but the tongue of the wise brings healing."* To tame the tongue, we must have a desire for better outcomes. The change will take effort, but with commitment, you can retrain your brain and live a life with much less regret. With a similar thought, John Newton

---

[1] Kerry Patterson and Al Switzler, *Crucial Conversations: Tools for Talking When the Stakes are High*, 3rd ed. (McGraw Hill, 2023).

said, "I am not the man I ought to be, I am not the man I wish to be, and I am not the man I hope to be, but, by the grace of God, I am not the man I used to be."[2]

A fool is quick-tempered, but a wise person stays calm when insulted. An honest witness tells the truth; a false witness tells lies. Some people make cutting remarks, but the words of the wise bring healing.
—Proverbs 12:16–18

[2] John Newton, "Quotable Quotes," Goodreads, accessed August 2025, https://www.goodreads.com/quotes/10750433-i-am-not-the-man-i-ought-to-be-i.

**PAUSE AND PONDER:
RECORD YOUR REFLECTIONS AND PERSONAL INSIGHTS.**

How about you? Do you tend to lash out, cutting the other person to the quick? Or does your tongue serve as a source of comfort leading to crucial conversations that bring healing and understanding to those you care for and serve?

CHAPTER 13:

Show Me Your Friends

There was a time in American culture when children played outside, running and riding throughout the neighborhood in pursuit of fun and adventure. Life was carefree, innocent, and without concern. Life was good.

Slowly but surely, fences appeared between yards; games were played inside on electronics; and invisible cocoons sheltered children from influences of the outside world. Families turned inward as fear became an underlying motivator for how life was to be navigated. Friendships suffered. Relationships waned as well-meaning helicopter parents hovered over their kids, prepared to intercept even the slightest threat of discomfort.

Their concerns were not entirely without warrant. Certainly, plenty of unbridled renegades exhibited great potential to pollute and corrupt the hearts and minds of otherwise "good kids."

In their efforts to shield children from the "wrong crowd," parents contributed to a lack of life skills that left children unprepared for the real world. In many ways, parents overcompensated and overcorrected against the ills they feared.

The antidote to fear is not to avoid people but to associate with the right posse. We can always choose the people we allow to influence our lives. Proverbs tells us that whoever walks with the wise becomes wiser, but the companion of fools will suffer harm. In other words, when you show me your friends, you show me your future. We do in fact become like those we hang around. Birds of a feather flock together. *"Bad company corrupts good character"* (1 Corinthians 15:33). It is fair to say that we are the average of our five closest friends.

We weren't designed to travel through life alone. We were made to be with each other. The key is not to hide but to decide who we want to run with. How about you? Take a look around. Who is influencing your life? Are the people you spend time with contributing to your success, or are they contributing to your demise? No one is perfect. We all have room for improvement. Getting to where you want to be in life has a lot to do with the people you do life with. Be careful not to let a loser tell you how to win. It is worth repeating: Show me your friends, and I'll show you your future.

Walk with the wise and become wise; associate with fools and get in trouble.
—Proverbs 13:20

PAUSE AND PONDER:
RECORD YOUR REFLECTIONS AND PERSONAL INSIGHTS.

How about you? How is your friend group influencing you? Are you a better person because of your friends? Do they encourage and inspire you to greater things? Do you have friends? Why or why not? What can you do to become a better friend? It is very likely that someone is looking for a friend like you.

CHAPTER 14:

All Smiles

A smile is a smile in any language. No matter where we find ourselves in the world, a smile translates. Smiles are meant to communicate happiness, pleasure, and delight. One smile often leads to another and often turns into laughter. It is hard to see a smile and not smile yourself. Smiles are easy to produce but hard to suppress when life is at its best. Smiles are powerful.

But not all smiles are the same. Some smiles present sadness in disguise. Many people suppress their hurt and tears with a smile, hoping to cover deep excruciating pain. Smiles can be deceiving. Sometimes, they serve as a deflector, not a reflector of reality. The smile on the surface shields us from the heartbreak inside.

Even in laughter, the heart may be aching. The words of Proverbs 14:13 reach through time and ring true in our lives today. We can relate. While we suffer in silence, we often suffer through smiles and forced laughter. Our happiness is manufactured. We fake our way through conversations in the hope of escaping to a place where our smile can give way to the frown that expresses the lingering ache within. The writer of Proverbs reminds us that there is a way that seems right, but in the end, it leads to ruin.

Faking it until you make it doesn't work when a smile should be a frown. Counterfeit smiles aren't sustainable. Often, the key to turning a frown into a smile lies in sharing with a trusted friend—someone who is willing to listen without judgment, pretense, or critique even though they may not have all the answers. We need that kind of friend. Better yet, we need to be that kind of friend.

> *Laughter can conceal a heavy heart, but when the laughter ends, the grief remains.*
>
> —Proverbs 14:13

PAUSE AND PONDER:
RECORD YOUR REFLECTIONS AND PERSONAL INSIGHTS.

How about you? Are you hurting beneath the surface? Have you been covering up the pain? Have you mastered the fabricated smile? Maybe it's time to take a risk and lean into a faithful friend who is willing to lend an ear and hold a confidence. Don't have a trusted friend? Start by becoming one, and don't be surprised if the friend you need will appear and turn your frown into a smile.

CHAPTER 15:

Is This How?

When you grow up in a highly dysfunctional family, abnormal is the norm. All too often, history repeats itself within the walls of homes that are cursed with chaos. The apple rarely falls far from the tree.

Dysfunction in chaotic families raises its head in many ways. Whether the dysfunction stems from the liquid courage of alcohol that promotes erratic behavior or enabling that traps souls in a cycle of codependency, the cycle of hurting people who hurt people repeats itself day in and day out for generations. The treadmill of emotional, mental, and physical delinquency is due in part to our nature and how we were nurtured. Many of our least desirable habits and hangups are knit into the fabric of our DNA. These innate tendencies are simply part of who we are. Other aspects of our persona have been learned by observation and the influence that others have had in our lives. Our behavior, mindset, and perspectives were shaped by the tribe from which we hail.

One such trait that prevailed in my house was a lack of self-control. Some might call it a free spirit; others might refer to it as freedom of expression or brutal honesty. In reality, it was selfish, childish rage that pounded hearts and heads when things didn't go as expected. If a point needed to be made, voices were raised. If emphasis was needed, things were thrown. If all else failed, physical force would be enlisted. It was ugly, angry, and wrong.

There was a better way, which was not put into practice in my family for generations. What might the outcome have been if somewhere, among the branches of my family tree, someone had learned to put King Solomon's words into practice? Words such as, *"A soft answer turns away wrath"* (Proverbs 15:1). Or *"A hot-tempered person starts fights; a cool-tempered person stops them."* (Proverbs 15:4). And perhaps the one needed most, *"A hot-tempered person starts fights; a cool-tempered person stops them"* (Proverbs 15:18).

I acknowledge that positive changes in behavior are not easy to make. It takes the Lord and a loving friend to help redirect the course that life might otherwise take. Although unlearning takes tremendous effort, it can be done.

Overcoming the tendency to lose one's cool is a major challenge, especially when one is entangled in intense conflict or conversation. Being told to calm down, act your age, or quit being like your abusive parent only serves to feed the flame. But a soft, gentle voice that is firm but caring can serve as a catalyst for interrupting the pattern that leads in the wrong direction. Simply by asking, "Is this how you want to handle this right now?" you can appeal to the person who is enraged in such a way as to calm the waters and point to a new and better approach.

> *A gentle answer deflects anger, but harsh words make tempers flare. . . . A hot-tempered person starts fights; a cool-tempered person stops them.*
>
> —Proverbs 15:1, 18

PAUSE AND PONDER:
RECORD YOUR REFLECTIONS AND PERSONAL INSIGHTS.

How about you? How far did the apple fall from your family tree? Course corrections can be made. You can justify your undesirable actions by claiming that this is just the way you are or just the way you were raised. Or you can take control of your life, invite the Lord and others to help you discover a better way that won't repeat your family history.

CHAPTER 16:

The Rhymes, Rhythms, and Routines of Life

There is a certain rhythm to life; it moves ahead with little notice. We are far more predicable than we realize; we eat, sleep, work, and repeat. We are truly creatures of habit. If we are lucky, we throw a little fun and adventure into the mix.

As predictable as life can become, some days come with a shocking surprise. The shock may be triggered by an unexpected call, a strange turn of events, or a tragic outcome that we had no way of knowing was in our future.

Life happens. We are part spectator and part participant. We feel as if we can control certain outcomes, but we have no control over others. Life is just that way; we experience ups, downs, and everything in between.

One day as I sat at my breakfast table enjoying a hot cup of coffee, the call came. My adult son who is in his late twenties called to say that one of his closest friends had just died of an acute heart attack. "It only takes one person to believe in you," he shared. His buddy had that kind of influence in his life. This reminded me that the opportunity to impact the life of another often comes when we least expect it—with an interruption in the everyday rhythm and grind of life. If we are honest, we take life for granted. We forget that we can be here one minute and gone the next. Life is predicable, until it's not.

Proverbs 16:9 reveals that a man plans his ways, but the Lord established his steps. In other words, we can map our life out and seek to hit the mark, but in the end, our days are numbered. We do well to make our plans and commit our ways to the Lord, realizing there will come a day when our plans come to an end. The routine and rhythm will cease to exist.

"*There is a path before each person that seems right, but it ends in death*" (Proverbs 14:12). Our decisions are not made in a vacuum; choices have consequences that are either good or bad. Blessed is the one who trusts in the Lord for His plans and purpose in life. As we navigate this journey we call life, there is no better way to travel than with a friend whose gracious words are like honeycomb—sweetness to the soul and health to the body.

Given the unpredictability that waits just around the curve, what a privilege it is to share our thoughts with those we love while they are still with us. If we aren't careful, we can miss the beautiful opportunity to be the one person who believes in the potential of another.

The greatest impact of our lives is often found in the simple interactions of daily life. Moment by moment, we have opportunities to impart lasting inspiration in the lives of others, reaching far beyond the years we walked together with those we love.

> *We can make our plans, but the LORD determines our steps.*
>
> —Proverbs 16:9

PAUSE AND PONDER:
RECORD YOUR REFLECTIONS AND PERSONAL INSIGHTS.

How about you? Who believed in you and helped shape who you have become? Who do you believe in? You can make your plans, but don't miss the plans the Lord has for you to be an influence with eternal impact in the life of another. Make your plans, but allow the Lord to direct your path. When you do, the rhymes, rhythms, and routines of your life will take on even greater meaning and purpose.

CHAPTER 17:

Drop the Jelly Jar

O ne of my favorite things about college was cramming for finals late at night before the big test. It wasn't hitting the books that I loved, it was the pizza.

Even now, I feel bad for the pizza delivery guy. Not only did we not tip very well, but sometimes, while he walked up four flights of stairs to deliver our pizza, one of us would run down a different set of stairs and rub grape jelly on his windshield. We would then watch as he struggled to see through the blurry windshield. More than one driver made the dreadful mistake of turning on their windshield wipers in an attempt to improve visibility. Epic fail. We were awful. Why? We were young and stupid.

Proverbs 17:1 reminds me of those days: *"Better a dry crust eaten in peace than a house filled with feasting— and conflict."* For the pizza delivery guy, we were troublemakers. We stirred up unnecessary conflict for a guy just trying to make ends meet.

During those college days, mornings often came too early, and breakfast was leftover dry pizza crust from the night before. I'd be lying if I didn't admit that I often reflected on our prank from the night before and felt a wave of guilt. We had feasted on late-night pizza while we stirred up conflict with an innocent, hardworking soul. The better choice would have been to eat our dry crust in peace and leave the pizza guy alone. We were terrible.

How many times have I done things that had the same effect but under different circumstances? Too many times, I have stirred the jar, smeared the jelly, and caused unnecessary strife in the life of others. Oh, that I would leave well enough alone. If only I had pursued peace and not insisted on making my point to win an argument. A dry crust eaten in peace is far better than gloating as I feast on my ability to articulate my perspective at the cost of unity, harmony, and broken relationships.

Although I graduated from college, I am still working to earn my degree in peacemaking. I hope to graduate with honors soon. To do so, I must practice humility, compassion, and thinking of others more than I think of myself. And certainly, I must give up the idea of making fun of someone at their expense. That is a must.

I can do better. Scripture is clear; it says, *"God blesses those who work for peace"* (Matthew 5:9). It is time for me to drop the jelly jar and start enjoying my dry crust eaten in peace.

> *Better a dry crust eaten in peace than a house filled with feasting—and conflict. . . . Those who mock the poor insult their Maker; those who rejoice at the misfortune of others will be punished.*
> —Proverbs 17:1, 5

PAUSE AND PONDER:
RECORD YOUR REFLECTIONS AND PERSONAL INSIGHTS.

How about you? How do people feel when you walk into the room? Are they inspired and encouraged, or are they resentful and full of regret? We have an opportunity to make the world a better place, and peacemaking is a great place to start.

CHAPTER 18:

Bitter Betrayal

Have you ever been betrayed? Maybe it was a close friend, family member, or favorite coworker. Regardless of the nature of the relationship, betrayal not only hurts, but it hurts bad.

At its root, betrayal is abandonment. It is especially painful when it comes from someone you have trusted and confided in.

There was a time when I worked to build a thriving organization in partnership with a very close friend. Together, we were making a difference in the lives of many people; we felt a sense of calling, purpose, and deep satisfaction in what we did. All seemed to be going well when one day, out of the blue, I was sucker-punched. I received notice that my friend was not only leaving the organization I had founded, but he was launching a new organization with the exact same mission and vision.

I was blindsided, devastated, shocked, and hugely disappointed. What went wrong? What had I done? What did I miss? I was caught totally off guard. I had no idea that for eight months prior to his departure, my friend had been secretly organizing a separate entity and had been working behind my back to take clients, associates, and key relationships with him. When I asked why, I was informed it was a necessary ending because he felt called to do his own thing. Really? At whose expense? I had been betrayed!

It took years for me to work through the emotional and mental stress related to that betrayal, not to mention the financial setbacks and challenges involved in rebuilding as years of momentum had been lost. Those close to the situation wondered what had happened. After all, weren't we close friends?

The writer of Proverbs speaks to the importance of genuine, devoted friendship when he says, "*There are 'friends' who destroy each other, but a real friend sticks closer than a brother*" (Proverbs 18:24).

The key descriptor? *Real friend.* I am convinced those who betray are not real friends. They are in reality "frenemies." They are more interested in self-preservation and self-interest than building deep and lasting relationships. A real friend sticks closer than a brother. A "frenemy" uses others to get what they want.

Having survived brutal betrayal, I have come to realize you can't make new old friends. I now cherish, more than ever, lasting friendships that have endured nearly a half century!

Strong friendships withstand the test of time. Even the best relationships require give and take, patience, commitment, and sacrifice. Great friendships are full of laughter, adventure, and a lot of heartfelt tears. It has been said that a real friend walks in when the rest of the world walks out. I have friends like that, and for them, I am forever grateful.

When I was betrayed, I was not left alone. Those who had seen me at my best and challenged me when I was at my worst, stepped in, stepped up and did as they had always done. They listened, comforted, and loved me through the other side of bitter and regrettable betrayal. The best part? They helped me learn how to forgive and release the one who had hurt me so deeply. To do otherwise would have been to live in a prison of the past. Forgiveness is the key to overcoming the grief and sadness brought on by betrayal.

How about you? Have you been betrayed? Is the pain of betrayal holding you hostage and keeping you from a future full of new opportunity and hope? Maybe it's time to release the past and embrace a new beginning.

If you have been the betrayer, today might be the perfect day to reach back in time and seek the forgiveness your heart needs.

There are "friends" who destroy each other, but a real friend sticks closer than a brother.
                                        —Proverbs 18:24

PAUSE AND PONDER:
RECORD YOUR REFLECTIONS AND PERSONAL INSIGHTS.

How about you? Have you been betrayed? Were you betrayed by someone you believed was a true friend? Have you set them free? If you hold onto a grudge or resentment, they will continue to control you. Consider forgiving them and setting yourself free from the pain of the past.

CHAPTER 19:

Counting Chickens

One of my favorite things about living on the prairie is the exposure we get to urban and rural aspects of life. While I have the privilege of serving Fortune 500 clients, I also have the unique opportunity to serve large agricultural endeavors in remote places.

The modern American farm is easy to underestimate. Yes, the products and services are very primal, but the way they operate is more like a NASA launch pad. Technology is at the heart of today's farming life.

One of my clients not only pays me well, but I rarely make a visit to west Texas without being sent home with at least two cartons of farm-fresh eggs. Trust me, there is a huge difference in between those eggs and the common variety found in the cooler of the local supermarket. If I have learned anything, it is that a clucking chicken is no guarantee of a scrambled egg. The hen can do her work, but it is up to the farmer and his customer to make sure that precious, fragile egg makes it to the frying pan.

Unfortunately, I have failed more than once at getting my delicate little cargo safely home. Because of the remote locations I visit, I often drive what many would consider a monster truck. My Ford F-250 is lifted seven inches higher than the standard factory model. Let's just say I have never been more aware of this height difference than when, in my excitement to share my fresh eggs with my wife, I rush the process and accidentally open my passenger door too quickly launching cartons of eggs skyward only to have them land on the unforgiving pavement. Each time, I thought I knew where my fragile little load was nestled. I was wrong. Humpty Dumpty did indeed have a fatal fall, and I have proof that eggs don't fly.

Proverbs 19:2 is a great reminder to not count your chickens before they hatch, or should I say, "Don't count your eggs before they are scrambled." The passage says, *Enthusiasm without knowledge is no good; haste makes mistakes.*

There isn't a businessperson alive who hasn't heard these fateful words: "The contract is signed, and the check is in the mail." These are exciting words to hear from a new client. It is easy to express enthusiasm until the check bounces! Proverbs proves true; enthusiasm without knowledge is no good.

We should be excited when we see the potential of a good deal and a great break. But the real celebration should take place only after the basketball goes through the hoop before the buzzer sounds. It's not over until it's over. It's not cooked until it's fried!

Be hopeful, anticipate the best, and look to the future with great expectation, but remember that too much enthusiasm, without adequate care and knowledge, has a way of slapping egg on your face. The next time you close a deal, experience a windfall, or hear of a trend that is in your favor, shake off the pom-poms, stretch your legs, and bend your knees in the ready position, but don't do a back flip until the plane has landed and everyone has made it to baggage claim! Don't count the clucks and all your bucks until the chicken is fried up in the pan. Proverbs got it right; enthusiasm without knowledge is no good.

> *Enthusiasm without knowledge is no good; haste makes mistakes.*
>
> —Proverbs 19:2

PAUSE AND PONDER:
RECORD YOUR REFLECTIONS AND PERSONAL INSIGHTS.

How about you? Have you been too optimistic? Have you put too much trust in yourself or the circumstances? Have you gotten ahead of God's plan with a few nudges of your own? An informed mind makes the best decision. How can you rely less on hunch and intuition?

CHAPTER 20:

Liquid Courage and the Yellow Line

L iquid courage leads to leaky ways. As a young boy I often found myself sitting on a bar stool in a dingy tavern as my dad threw back bottle after bottle of beer. The more he drank, the louder he became. The louder he became, the more likely the night would end in a bar fight.

More than once, I had a front row seat as a ringside spectator to an all-out brawl. Sometimes, my dad would come out on top; other times, he would stumble to the car, toss me the keys as he was passing out, and tell me to keep my eyes on the highway's yellow line to get us safely home. This was quite an adventure for a ten-year-old boy who could barely see over the steering wheel as he strained to point his toes toward the gas pedal of an old Ford Galaxy 500.

The winding road led us home. He usually slept it off in the back seat as I made my way to the security of my twin bed in the room I shared with my younger brother. If we were lucky, he would wake up near dawn, throwing up his guts. If things turned for the worse, he would drag himself into the house and, as if he heard the sound of the boxing ring bell, he would find a reason to lay into my mother like he had with his so-called bar buddy. Either way, it was hell.

My dad has passed now. We survived his bout with alcohol and us. It was rough. The memories are bad. And the outcome? My mother, my brother, and I are nothing short of living miracles because we made it through.

Proverbs 20:1 serves as a great warning of alcohol's potential for inviting trouble. The verse says, *"Wine produces mockers; alcohol leads to brawls. Those led astray by drink cannot be wise."* My experience with liquid courage caused me to become a teetotaler. For me, it's just not worth the risk. No one knows the point at which a cucumber becomes a pickle. Until someone can tell me when a drinker becomes a drunk, I will be leaving an empty seat open at the bar.

That yellow line remains vivid in my mind. To this day I do all I can not to cross it. Liquid courage and the yellow line don't mix. Living and driving sober has served me well as my courage comes from a much higher power.

> *Wine produces mockers; alcohol leads to brawls. Those led astray by drink cannot be wise.*
> —Proverbs 20:1

**PAUSE AND PONDER:
RECORD YOUR REFLECTIONS AND PERSONAL INSIGHTS.**

How about you? How has alcohol impacted your life? Has it ever caused you trouble? Have you ever considered what it might be like to live without it? What risks are associated with strong drink?

CHAPTER 21:

Ready to Rumble?

Who doesn't enjoy a good fight? Hardly anyone. Fights are stressful, rarely helpful; unfortunately, they are part of life.

Not all fights are full of fists; some are just all out fits. Some are passive. Others are aggressive.

Fights can bring healing, but most of the time, they compound hurt. That reminds me of the ole saying, "A bulldog can whip a skunk, but it's not worth the stink."

I think the writer of Proverbs had a similar thought in mind when he made this observation about quarrelsome behavior: *"It's better to live alone in the corner of an attic than with a quarrelsome wife in a lovely home"* (Proverbs 21:9). And then again, later in the chapter, he says, *"It's better to live alone in the desert than with a quarrelsome, complaining wife"* (Proverbs 21:19). Now, the ladies are getting a bad rap here. The real question is what is causing all the quarreling. Yes, she could be the issue, but most than likely, there is plenty of blame to go around.

James 4:1 probes at the cause of quarrels. *"What is causing the quarrels and fights among you? Don't they come from the evil desires at war within you?"* Now we are getting somewhere. Let's get to the bottom of the problem. According to James, the source of quarrels is that we want something, and we don't get it. So, what do we do? We fight for it. Yup, good ole selfishness has raised its ugly head.

The next time you get into a quarrel with your spouse, a friend, a service provider, or the man upstairs, ask yourself, "What am I fighting for?" Are you fighting for the greater good or simply because you aren't getting what you want?

Let's recognize the source of the quarrels among us. Rather than being the one found at the end of our index finger, perhaps it is the one to which that finger is attached.

Conflict is coming. The opportunity to fuss and fight finds its way into our lives every day. Let's become more aware of the role we can play as a peacemaker not a troublemaker. There are times when we should stand up for something worth fighting for. There are also times when mercy, grace, and love can save a whole lot of hurt, resentment, and broken relationships.

Are you ready to rumble? You can choose to live in the attic or all alone in the desert, or you can look for ways to give more of yourself and grab less of your selfish desires. Life is just better when we set selfishness aside. Put down the gloves and reach for a hug!

It's better to live alone in the corner of an attic than with a quarrelsome wife in a lovely home.

—Proverbs 21:9

It's better to live alone in the desert than with a quarrelsome, complaining wife.

—Proverbs 21:19

PAUSE AND PONDER:
RECORD YOUR REFLECTIONS AND PERSONAL INSIGHTS.

How about you? Do you know someone who is a nag? Is it possible that others consider you to be a nag? What is the source of all the nagging? Is there something you want that is at the center of the nagging? Can you define it and address it? How can you get to the source?

CHAPTER 22:

What Are You Known For?

When people hear your name, what is the first thing they think? It has been said that each of us is five people: Who we think people think we are. Who people think we are. Who people think we think we are. Who we think we are. And who the Creator knows we are.

Who are you? What is your reputation? Proverbs 22:1 says we choose our reputation. We have a say in the matter; it doesn't just happen. What we say and do play a large part in shaping the reputation we build. Sometimes, being less than our best has a way of influencing our reputation the most. It only takes one bad choice to detract from your reputation. A great reputation takes work and is developed over time.

Everyone knows somebody who was loved, respected, and admired by others and, for whatever reason, they made a bad choice, had a lapse in judgment, or displayed a lack of integrity that compromised their reputation in an instance.

Of course, no one is perfect. No one is everything they seem. Nothing is ever as good as it appears. We can fret and worry about what people think, or we can do our best to be who we truly are.

Pressure reveals the person. Time will tell. Who we are will eventually be made clear. The key is to build our reputation on the decisions we make every day. Character and a reputation are built in the acts of everyday life. It is true that the reputation we make is the reputation we choose. Choose today who you want to be and the reputation you desire to build. The choice is yours.

> *Choose a good reputation over great riches; being held in high esteem is better than silver or gold.*
> —Proverbs 22:1

PAUSE AND PONDER:
RECORD YOUR REFLECTIONS AND PERSONAL INSIGHTS.

How about you? Have you ever stopped to consider what it might be like to be on the other side of you? Would you want to be around you? What are you doing to ensure that you maintain a good reputation? Are you participating in anything that could jeopardize your reputation?

CHAPTER 23:

Time to Quit?

A good portion of life is spent in a regular routine. We eat sleep, work, and repeat. Not much thought is given to the everyday rhythms of life. It is what it is. We get by with little incident.

However, there are days when circumstances, accidents, opportunities, or happenings erupt outside our control. The regular pattern of ordinary life is interrupted with something extraordinary, and a memorable moment is hatched, or an unusual experience is born.

Surprises have a way of sneaking up on us. Some are good, and some are tragic. Things are moving along predictably and then suddenly, boom! Life happens. We are shaken from our nook, and the world suddenly splashes cold water in our faces.

They said there would be days like these—days when the control we thought we had is lost in the reality that we are simply along for the ride in many ways. The sun rises and the sun sets. Another twenty-four hours pass, and we live through yet another average day.

Sure, we get to pick and choose a few treats from the candy store of life at times, but in large part, we have little to say about where the world is heading and where we find ourselves in the bigger scheme of things. One thing leads to another, and eventually we wake up where we are.

We can continue to float like a dead fish down a lazy river, or we can quit accepting the so-called cards that we have been dealt, reshuffle the deck, and play a different hand. Folding isn't an option. We may not be in control, but we certainly can influence the outcome. Doing nothing changes nothing. It's time that we quit the blame game and start doing what we can do to move the needle on the dashboard of life.

One lazy Saturday afternoon, I found myself lounging like a couch potato, doing nothing but wasting time. As I dozed off and on like a hound dog on a warm sunny afternoon, and I did my fair share of channel surfing. I landed on an interview with a prominent rock star who was asked what gave him the courage to pursue his dream. His response took this "couch potato" straight out of the oven. He said, "I never wanted to be that guy who said he wished he would've, could've, or should've."

Sometimes, we must quit what we are doing in pursuit of what we are called to accomplish in life. All too often, we settle. We know we are meant for more, but the comfort and tranquility of the couch holds us back from the life we were meant to live. We accept the gold watch, pack our office into a file box, and hope we live long enough in retirement to make it all worth it.

Life allows us to accommodate passivity, but it also has a way of responding to action when we take responsibility for ourselves. It comes down to what we accept and expect. We can allow the status quo to prevail, and little will change, or we can decide to quit accepting less than the best and begin expecting things to get better.

Proverbs 23:4 says, *"Be wise enough to know when to quit."* What are we holding onto? What have we come to accept? Has comfort crept in and convinced you that you are powerless? Have you given up just about the time a breakthrough is breaking out?

Sometimes, we quit too soon, but other times, we don't quit soon enough. We hang onto the past, bad habits, poor self-esteem, and the way things have always been, assuming and expecting things will somehow change if we just shift life into neutral and let the engine idle.

Is it time to quit? Is it time to let go of attitudes, mindsets, and ways of thinking that are holding you back? Is that dead-end job robbing you of the life you always dreamed of? The potential we dream of is possible. We can play a significant role in the life we've been given.

Yes, much has been decided, and we have been placed in a time and space not of our choosing. But we can make a difference in the ultimate outcome if we decide to quit accepting the status quo and start expecting things to change as we move into action and live responsibly.

> *Don't wear yourself out trying to get rich. Be wise enough to know when to quit.*
> —Proverbs 23:4

PAUSE AND PONDER:
RECORD YOUR REFLECTIONS AND PERSONAL INSIGHTS.

How about you? Have you ever considered that quitting might lead to what you are seeking? Is there anything holding you back from the life you are called to live? What role does faith play? Is uncertainty holding you back? Can you think of anyone God has used who didn't face uncertainty? It is impossible to please him without faith. Don't let fear keep you from God's best.

CHAPTER 24:

Pressure Is Coming

Pressure reveals the person. What happens when you get squeezed? What comes out? The inside comes out when the outside gets to you.

In high school sports, I was Mr. Average. I was at the top of the B-team and at the bottom of the A-team. For one game I was allowed to travel with the best players to an away game with an archrival.

As it turns out, we had a major lead with thirty seconds left in the game. Everyone had been in the game except for one player, me! I leaned back on the bench hoping the coach would forget that I existed. Afterall, how would I impact the monster lead with so little time left on the clock.

I failed at hide-and-seek. I was put in the game and given the ball. I was under major pressure to dribble the full length of the court without losing the ball and losing my dignity. I lost both. All was well until I got to half-court. It was at this point that I stumbled and kicked the basketball to the other end of the court. The crowd roared in laughter as my heart sank, and the buzzer went off. The game was over and in less than thirty seconds, I made a fool out of myself. I had caved under pressure. It was embarrassing. The circumstances confirmed what the coach and I already knew; when it came to basketball, I wasn't championship material. Pressure revealed the player.

When have you failed under pressure? We all have moments when we are less than our best. Sometimes, we reach a breaking point that is much more serious than my embarrassing failure in a basketball game. Sometimes, real-life pressure mounts, and we lose it and not in a good way.

When is enough, enough? What is your breaking point? Everyone has a point at which they have had enough. Where does your tolerance end? What is to be tolerated, and where does patience end? Is the line that gets crossed subjective? When is action required? Is abdication ever the right answer, or is that to be avoided at all costs?

Self-control plays a role when it comes to how we respond under pressure. The more we have, the more power we have over the circumstances. The less self-control we have, the more the circumstances control us. Being self-aware and recognizing our tendencies, patterns, and likelihoods can help us prepare for the pressure that comes. We know what to expect.

People are like oranges, grapefruits and lemons; when squeezed, they leak. One thing is for sure; pressure brings the juice—sweet, sour, or somewhere in between. People are sure to get a taste of who we are when our lives are under pressure.

Pressure is coming. It is part of life. What comes out when we are under pressure can be determined today as we prepare for the squeeze that is sure to come. Proverbs 24:10 says, *"If you fail under pressure, your strength is too small."*

Strength training must begin today if we are to be ready for the pressures that are certain to come. How we hold up under pressure is no accident. It simply reveals the person we have become.

> *If you fail under pressure, your strength is too small.*
> —Proverbs 24:10

PAUSE AND PONDER:
RECORD YOUR REFLECTIONS AND PERSONAL INSIGHTS.

How about you? When do you feel pressured? How do you react when under pressure? How can you gain control of your reactions and responses when life heats up? Consider in advance how you want to respond and decide now to make it happen.

CHAPTER 25:

Apples of Gold

In the 1990s Senator Robert Byrd shared a beautiful passage from the floor of the United States Senate as he encouraged his fellow senators to speak with compassion, eloquence, and kindness. As a Senate staffer, I experienced his admonishment firsthand. His timely words have stayed with me for years. He shared Proverbs 25:11, which says, *"Like apples of gold in settings of silver is a word aptly spoken"* (TLV).

Following Senator Byrd's wise words brings life to ourselves and others. As we look in the mirror each day, we come face to face with an opportunity to affirm who we are in the eyes of God. We are cherished, loved, and pursued by Him. As we recognize the love He has for us, we are equipped to carry apples of love in settings of silver to those we engage with throughout the day.

Sharing apples of gold not only brings joy to our lives, but it also brightens the day and lightens the load of those we meet. But not every day is golden. Everybody struggles to endure the challenges of bad days.

During our day-to-day interaction, we tend to only see the tip of the iceberg of the challenges people are experiencing. We rarely know what people are really going through. There is so much more going on below the surface, and not all of that is peachy, positive, and packed with pleasure. Most likely, much of it is just the opposite. Sometimes, smiles and positive attitudes hide the reality of excruciating pain as people struggle to navigate life's tension. Their smiles and "positive" attitudes fade as the reality of their sadness sets in and they are alone with themselves. It is then that the masks come off.

By having an understanding, empathetic, and encouraging attitude, we can extend the benefit of the doubt to others; we can choose to be empathetic and love deeper even if the other person doesn't ask or think they need empathy. When we lead with love and mercy, grace follows. Giving someone a break, a second chance, or a word of affirmation rarely goes unnoticed. It may, in fact, save a life. Opportunities to serve as a ray of light, hope, and positive energy, surround us.

We have a choice to make each morning: We can be a buzzard or a butterfly. We tend to get what we are looking for. A buzzard looks for death, destruction, and demise. A butterfly looks for nectar, nobility, and nourishment. We possess the power to ravage or redeem.

Colossians 4:5–6 highlights and affirms the *"apples of gold"* mindset. It encourages us to make the most of every opportunity we have as we participate in gracious conversation, which attracts others to the joy set before us and the light that lives within us. When distributing apples of gold becomes our passion, we have truly gained a deeper understanding of our mission and calling in life.

How sweet it is to be loved as the apple of His eye as we serve as His ambassadors of hope, faith, and love. Share an apple today!

> *Timely advice is lovely, like golden apples in a silver basket.*
>
> —Proverbs 25:11

PAUSE AND PONDER:
RECORD YOUR REFLECTIONS AND PERSONAL INSIGHTS.

How about you? Do you know someone who is like Senator Byrd? Do you know someone who offers timely advice? Have you every thanked them for their role in your life? How can you become someone who serves as an encouragement to others?

CHAPTER 26:

Ignore Ignorance

A s my mother always said, "In the word *ignorance* is the word *ignore*. Ignore ignorance."
You have to play it smart when dealing with fools. To respond or not to respond . . . that is the question. Say what, or say not? Recognizing the level of gravity associated with the circumstance is the key to deciding on a wise response or no response at all.

Fools don't know what they don't know, or they care little about knowing the difference. They are wise in their own eyes and care little about what is right or wrong so long as they get what they want. In the end, fools are the ultimate contributor to their own demise.

It is difficult to know whether to engage with a fool or simply shake your head and walk away. Proverbs 26:4 can leave you scratching your head unless you learn to weigh the way to deal with the fool.

> *"Don't answer the foolish arguments of fools, or you will become as foolish as they are.*
> —Proverbs 26:4

**PAUSE AND PONDER:
RECORD YOUR REFLECTIONS AND PERSONAL INSIGHTS.**

How about you? Do you have someone in your life that you are allowing to get under your skin? What if you simply determined to ignore their foolishness and didn't give them the time of day? You don't have to be right, but you don't have to participate in stupidity either.

CHAPTER 27:

Bag the Bragging

When I was a teenager, there was a man in town who drove around in a pickup truck and wearing a cowboy hat. All the while, he pretended that he was talking on his cell phone. He had a strong desire to look and feel important. The only problem was everyone knew that the telephone he held in his hand was nothing more than the handle from an abandoned home telephone. I suppose you could say he was a "big talker."

Everybody knows a big talker. A big talker can't share a story without embellishment and making himself part of the storyline, but nothing is ever as it seems. The victories are sweeter than the tasting confirms, the obstacles are larger than the picture painted, and the grass is always greener and lusher than the mower requires.

In truth, the big talker is all hat and no cattle. They've got the look but nothing to really show for it. A cowboy hat doesn't make you any more of a wrangler than a hammer makes you a master carpenter. The big talker is a bragger. He talks a lot about what is going to be, what is about to happen, the fortune he is about to make, the ship that is about to come in, and what a big day tomorrow will be.

He may not come right out and say it, but it is always implied. Look at me! Watch me! See what I'm doing. Aren't I awesome? I bet you wish you had what I've got. But it's all a bunch of wind. A good look under the hood reveals the four-cylinder engine doesn't match the dragster size wheels and flaming decals. He's a poser, a fake, and a fraud.

Proverbs 27:1–2 makes it clear that it's time to bag the bragging. If you have to tell people how great you are, then you're probably not. Let your actions speak for you. The proof is in the pudding not the size of the hat.

Don't brag about tomorrow, since you don't know what the day will bring. Let someone else praise you, not your own mouth—a stranger, not your own lips.
—Proverbs 27:1–2

PAUSE AND PONDER:
RECORD YOUR REFLECTIONS AND PERSONAL INSIGHTS.

How about you? Are you looking for recognition or seeking praise to the point that you tend to brag on your accomplishments? When was the last time you intentionally bragged on someone else?

CHAPTER 28:

In Pursuit of Meaningful Work

We have all met someone we consider to be a starving artist. We admire their free spirit and passion for chasing their dream, but we rarely admire their pocketbook.

Where is the balance? In Western culture, we have an ideal that leans into the idea that we have a right to pursue a means of making a living that is satisfying and brings us pleasure. We even equate our level of satisfaction and enjoyment with God's will. This is a dangerous concept. There has never been a guarantee of comfort in a calling. The joy is not found in the work but in the one who provides the opportunity to put our hand to the plow.

Having a fulfilling job is outstanding; some people are even fortunate enough to see their work as worship. Work provides an opportunity to fulfill our calling. It is not simply a means to an end but a means by which we can express our gratitude for provision and our calling to know Him and make Him known. But if we are not careful, work can become an idol.

Much of the world wakes up every morning with one thing on their mind, "What can I do to feed my family today?" Such a thought is foreign to many who navigate lanes of traffic on their way to high-rise buildings on the horizon. It is not wrong to pursue career opportunities, but it is wrong to place our hope in the wads of currency that line our purses.

We do well to consider how we are gifted in our pursuit of meaningful work. What talents do we possess that put us in a unique position to maximize who we were designed to be? We have an obligation to the creator to steward our abilities and our influence to the max. Settling for a less challenging career in order to satisfy our desire for recreation and pleasure would be tragic.

The Lord is less concerned about what we do than how we do it. He has a "whatever" attitude. Colossians 3:17 gives us a hint, *"And whatever you do or say, do it as a representative of the Lord Jesus, giving thanks through him to God the Father."* Did you catch it? The key word is *whatever.*

The key to meaningful work and satisfaction in our careers is to realize that whatever we do has huge potential to be used by God for His purpose. He desires to have His kids playing on all kinds of playgrounds. He wants us to enjoy our work, but getting hung up on whether to swing from the monkey bars or slide down a slide is less of a concern. The key is to jump into the sandbox and enjoy the day with others.

If we aren't careful, we can start chasing fantasies and ideals that wear us out in pursuit of pampering our philosophies on meaningful work. Of course, there is nothing wrong with loving what you do, but if loving what you do isn't focused on serving as a representative of the King, then no amount of work or career choice will bring lasting fulfillment. We will miss the meaning of work.

Proverbs 28:19 nails it: *"A hard worker has plenty of food, but a person who chases fantasies ends up in poverty."* Is your plate empty and your bank account low? Make sure you aren't chasing fantasies in pursuit of an ideal and an idol, otherwise known as job satisfaction. Maybe it is time to roll up your sleeves, take hold of the plow, and look for the Lord to use you in whatever way He makes available. Such is not a compromise but rather an act of faith knowing that opportunity leads to opportunity. Work is good. Before we know it, that job flipping burgers turns into a management position, and the next thing we know, we're leading the entire restaurant chain.

God has a way of turning our humility into success. True success isn't found in chasing fantasies or in the number of zeros on our paychecks. True satisfaction is found in knowing whatever we choose to do brings honor to Him wherever He leads. "Wherever He Leads I'll Go," is not just a classic hymn; it is also a great way to approach life. Let's get going with meaningful work.

> *A hard worker has plenty of food, but a person who chases fantasies ends up in poverty.*
> —Proverbs 28:19

PAUSE AND PONDER:
RECORD YOUR REFLECTIONS AND PERSONAL INSIGHTS.

How about you? Is what you are doing the highest and best use of your time? Is your passion and talent producing the livelihood you desire? How can you know for certain that you aren't obsessed with a fantasy that might never become a reality? Do you have a sense of calling on your life? Are you willing to go wherever the Lord leads, even if there is no guarantee of comfort in in His calling?

CHAPTER 29:

Fear Not

I grew up in a home where rage was the norm. Fueled by alcohol and dysfunction, our house was a living hell when my dad came home drunk. Terror was the lingering atmosphere that prevailed. For as long as I can remember, my dad lacked self-control. He was often out of his mind like a rabid dog unleashed to ravage his prey. We lived in a house of horror. My mother took the brunt of his beatings and when he turned on us, she finally had enough. My dad became a convicted felon after he had tried, not once but twice, to take our lives.

It is fair to say that I understand what it means to live in fear. But if I learned anything from such a volatile environment, it is that fear is a choice. Danger is real. Fear is an option that rarely contributes to overcoming the presence of peril. I did not suppress my fear. I overcame it. Like David, the shepherd boy, I faced my giant, and he fell.

Psalms 27:1–2 gives a great prospective:

The Lord is my light and my salvation—so why should I be afraid? The Lord is my fortress, protecting me from danger, so why should I tremble? When evil people come to devour me, when my enemies and my foes attack me, they will stumble and fall.

We don't need to be foolish or reckless, and we would be wise to acknowledge that dangerous people do exist. But for the most part, we give too much credence to the people who try to use fear to intimidate, manipulate, and dominate our lives. If abuse is present, we owe it to ourselves to walk away. Self-respect requires that we not serve as doormats on the steps of a perpetrator. Nonetheless, fear is not mandatory. But courage is required.

With the Lord at our side, we need not fear. Our confidence is found in His strength, His wisdom, and His presence. When danger is present, we need not fear for He is near. Proverbs 29:25 gets it right: "*Fearing people is a dangerous trap, but trusting the LORD means safety.*"

Joshua 1:9 puts a bow on it: "*This is my command—be strong and courageous! Do not be afraid or discouraged. For the LORD your God is with you wherever you go.*"

There you have it: Fear not. Take courage. Trust the Lord, for he is with you.

Fearing people is a dangerous trap, but trusting the LORD means safety.
—Proverbs 29:25

How about you? What are you afraid of? What is the worst thing that could happen? Is real danger present? How can you be mindful of your safety without living in fear? What needs to change?

CHAPTER 30:

When Is Enough, Enough?

How much do we need? Where is the line between want and need?

At the click of a button, the consumer in me launches a porch full of packages. Getting what we want has never been easier. We don't even have to leave our houses to shop. The hunt is over. If we want it, we get it. Click, click, click! Convenience fuels our consumption. Before we know it, empty boxes fill our rooms, yet leave us empty and craving more.

Proverbs 30:8–9 is a great reminder of the need for balance:

Give me neither poverty nor riches! Give me just enough to satisfy my needs. For if I grow rich, I may deny you and say, "Who is the Lord?" And if I am too poor, I may steal and thus insult God's holy name.

Enough already! We stockpile gadgets galore as we hunt for more. We convince ourselves we need something, and within a few days, the latest and greatest acquisition is gathering dust, and we have to buy a new duster to care for our stockpile. While many in the world struggle to make ends meet, we struggle with where to store our junk, formerly known as something we need or must have.

Oh, Lord, teach us to be content! Help us realize that things were never meant to satisfy. Although there is nothing wrong with owning something nice, we must be careful that nice things don't start to own us.

The Apostle Paul must have just finished his daily devotion in Proverbs when he was inspired to write Philippians 4:11–13:

> *Not that I was ever in need, for I have learned how to be content with whatever I have. I know how to live on almost nothing or with everything. I have learned the secret of living in every situation, whether it is with a full stomach or empty, with plenty or little. For I can do everything through Christ, who gives me strength.*

Contentment is a beautiful thing. Consumerism is haunting. May the Lord strengthen our resolve and enlighten our better judgment as we consider the balance between our needs and wants.

Self is rarely satisfied by the things of this world. Things are not all bad, but we must learn that lasting satisfaction comes by being consumed by our love for the Lord. When we have Him, we have little need for anything else.

> *First, help me never to tell a lie. Second, give me neither poverty nor riches! Give me just enough to satisfy my needs. For if I grow rich, I may deny you and say, "Who is the LORD?" And if I am too poor, I may steal and thus insult God's holy name*
>
> —Proverbs 30:8–9

PAUSE AND PONDER:
RECORD YOUR REFLECTIONS AND PERSONAL INSIGHTS.

How about you? What is the difference between wants and needs? Is there anything wrong with desiring more than you need? Where is the balance?

CHAPTER 31:

Silence Is Agreement

S peak up. Find your voice. Silence is agreement. There are times when we do well to simply sit in silence, but there are also times when we must rise to the occasion and speak to the issue at hand.

We sat at the indoor soccer game enjoying the little league hopefuls running back and forth on the artificial grass. As they burned calories and battled for the ball, a screeching noise persisted behind the bleachers. Somewhere amongst a bay of arcade games, a malfunctioning electronic gaming box was having a fit. It was off the rails, blasting sound effects as it was stuck in action mode. It wasn't just loud. It was supersonic.

The soccer game continued as parent after parent would turn their heads toward the distraction. It was annoying, disruptive, and obnoxious. Surely someone who worked at the facility would attend to the problem. Nothing happened. Nobody moved. The crowd focused their senses and overlooked the obvious. Everyone ignored the problem. Except one . . . Me!

It was time for someone to speak up—to do something. We had gone from looking at the problem to looking at each other. Everyone was wondering who would do something about the problem. There were no elections or drawing of straws to pick a leader. Everyone just sat there accepting the situation, passively marking time tolerating the annoyance.

Finally, I couldn't take it anymore. I stood to my feet, walked to the arcade, located the problem, and pulled the plug. Problem solved. Issue resolved. There was peace in the valley once again. Applause and praise were extended as the soccer game ended.

It seemed obvious that someone needed to speak up, take action, and try to make a difference. But no one found a way. Everyone accepted the situation.

But why? Were they deaf, oblivious, or sensorially deficient? Had they decided it was none of their business, not their problem, or someone else's responsibility? Were they just lazy, unmotivated, or too tired to care? Maybe they felt unqualified, unprepared, or incapable. Amazingly, no one—including me—even tried until I couldn't take it anymore.

I was no hero. I was simply at my wits end. Somebody had to do something and because nobody did, I became the reluctant problem solver. No medals were awarded. No lives were changed and based on reactions, hardly anybody noticed.

Speaking up isn't always the right thing to do. Sometimes, it is easy. Other times, it is hard to muster the courage to stand in the gap. Proverbs 31:8–9 says there is a time when we must find our voice and speak up. We can't look to others. We have to step in, show up, and speak out. In those moments, we must reject passivity, take responsibility, and speak up when it matters most.

A malfunctioning arcade is nothing compared to the injustices and social ills that surround us each day. We must find a way. We must find our voice, and we must speak up and take a stand. If we don't, who will? When we show up and speak up, there is high probability that things will be changed because we took the initiative and spoke up.

> *Speak up for those who cannot speak for themselves; ensure justice for those being crushed. Yes, speak up for the poor and helpless, and see that they get justice.*
>
> —Proverbs 31:8–9

PAUSE AND PONDER:
RECORD YOUR REFLECTIONS AND PERSONAL INSIGHTS.

How about you? It is one thing to see. It is another to notice. Who has the Lord brought into your life that you can influence and impact for good? No doubt you aren't called to be all things to all people, but how are you uniquely gifted to make a difference in the lives of some?

Acknowledgments and Special Thanks

To the love of my life, Stephanie. You have always believed in me, encouraged me, and loved me unconditionally. Thanks for letting Jesus use you in my life. You are truly my junior Holy Spirit.

To my wonderful children, Lauren-Elaine, Olivia-Christine, Joshua, Isaac, Emily-Rose, and Sophia-Rae. You have taught me more about life than you will ever know. And to the grandbabies: You bring Papa Bear so much joy! I pray you will learn great life lessons as you turn the pages of this book.

To my mother, Patsy Ann. You have been the anchor through many storms. Your love never fails. I am forever grateful that you chose life!

A special thanks to you, my readers. Thanks for joining me on this journey. I hope to hear from you. Contact me at www. raysanders.com. Don't be shy, I would love to hear the insights you gained as you pondered the Proverbs and explored what in the world King Solomon was thinking.

About the Author

Ray Sanders is the founder and CEO of Coaching Leaders, an executive coaching and revenue-generating business consulting firm that partners with Fortune 500 executives, CEOs, entrepreneurs, and business owners to help them navigate the challenges and opportunities that come with growing their companies and strengthening their leadership teams (raysanders.com).

As a CEO, Ray has grown multimillion-dollar organizations, advanced national and international brands, led a financial institution, served in a nonpartisan role with the United States Senate, led print and broadcast organizations, and pioneered initiatives to bring clean water to remote regions of the world. His leadership experience spans more than forty years.

Ray is recognized by his peers as a leader of leaders, a whiteboard aficionado, and an innovative growth strategist with a passion for purpose-driven cultures and values-based leadership development. His business coaching, mentoring, and personal ministry have given him a unique perspective on the wide range of struggles leaders face in all walks of life.

A skilled communicator, Ray has served as editor in chief for Oklahoma's largest weekly news journal, hosted an award-winning radio program, and been a keynote speaker for conventions, conferences, and campuses. He has published more than 150 articles and feature stories in print and online publications, including *The Baptist Messenger*, *The Oklahoman*, the Oklahoma Press Association, and others. Ray holds a BA degree from the University of Oklahoma.

Ray and his wife, Stephanie, are the founders of Edify Leaders, a nonprofit organization that inspires and mobilizes leaders to use their influence to impact the world for good (edifyleaders. org). While Ray continues to lead a thriving business in the marketplace, he also dedicates much of his time to speaking and leading ministry coaches who encourage hundreds of ministry leaders as they navigate the challenges of life and ministry.

A world traveler, Ray enjoys exploring new places with the love of his life, Stephanie. Together, they have six grown children and ten grandchildren.